THE
BURIAL
of the
DEAD

Rites I & II

MOREHOUSE PUBLISHING

NOTE:

The liturgy for the dead is an Easter liturgy. It finds all its meaning in the resurrection. Because Jesus was raised from the dead, we, too, shall be raised.

The liturgy, therefore, is characterized by joy, in the certainty that "neither death, nor life, nor angels, no principalities, nor things present, nor things to come, nor powers, nor height, nor depth, nor anything else in all creation, will be able to separate us from the love of God in Christ Jesus our Lord."

This joy, however, does not make human grief unchristian. The very love we have for each other in Christ brings deep sorrow when we are parted by death. Jesus himself wept at the grave of his friend. So, while we rejoice that one we love has entered into the nearer presence of our Lord, we sorrow in sympathy with those who mourn.

The texts in this edition of *The Burial of the Dead: Rites I & II* conform to the texts approved for the 1979 edition of *The Book of Common Prayer.*

Morehouse Publishing
P.O. Box 1321
Harrisburg, PA 17105

ISBN: 0-8192-1766-2

A catalog record for this book is available from
the Library of Congress.

The Burial of the Dead: Rite One

All stand while one or more of the following anthems is sung or said.

I am the resurrection and the life, saith the Lord;
he that believeth in me, though he were dead, yet shall he live;
and whosoever liveth and believeth in me shall never die.

I know that my Redeemer liveth,
and that he shall stand at the latter day upon the earth;
and though this body be destroyed, yet shall I see God;
whom I shall see for myself and mine eyes shall behold,
and not as a stranger.

For none of us liveth to himself,
and no man dieth to himself.
For if we live, we live unto the Lord;
and if we die, we die unto the Lord.
Whether we live, therefore, or die, we are the Lord's.

Blessed are the dead who die in the Lord;
even so saith the Spirit, for they rest from their labors.

The Celebrant says one of the following Collects, first saying

          The Lord be with you.
People   And with thy spirit.
Celebrant Let us pray.

At the Burial of an Adult

O God, whose mercies cannot be numbered: Accept our prayers on behalf of thy servant *N.*, and grant *him* an entrance into the land of light and joy, in the fellowship of thy saints; through Jesus Christ thy Son our Lord, who liveth and reigneth with thee and the Holy Spirit, one God, now and for ever. *Amen.*

At the Burial of a Child

O God, whose beloved Son did take little children into his arms and bless them: Give us grace, we beseech thee, to entrust this child *N.* to thy never-failing care and love, and bring us all to thy heavenly kingdom; through the same thy Son Jesus Christ our Lord, who liveth and reigneth with thee and the Holy Spirit, one God, now and for ever. *Amen.*

The people sit.

One or more of the following passages from Holy Scripture is read. If there is to be a Communion, a passage from the Gospel always concludes the Readings.

From the Old Testament

Isaiah 25:6-9 (He will swallow up death in victory)
Isaiah 61:1-3 (To comfort all that mourn)
Lamentations 3:22-26, 31-33 (The Lord is good unto them
   that wait for him)
Wisdom 3:1-5, 9 (The souls of the righteous are in the hand of God)
Job 19:21-27a (I know that my Redeemer liveth)

After the Old Testament Lesson, a suitable canticle or one of the following Psalms may be sung or said

Psalm 42 *Quemadmodum*

Like as the hart desireth the water-brooks, *
   so longeth my soul after thee, O God.

My soul is athirst for God, yea, even for the living God; *
   when shall I come to appear before the presence of God?

My tears have been my meat day and night, *
   while they daily say unto me, Where is now thy God?

Now when I think thereupon, I pour out my heart by myself; *
   for I went with the multitude, and brought them forth into
         the house of God;

In the voice of praise and thanksgiving, *
   among such as keep holy-day.

Why art thou so full of heaviness, O my soul? *
   and why art thou so disquieted within me?

O put thy trust in God; *
   for I will yet thank him, which is the help of my
         countenance, and my God.

Psalm 46 *Deus noster refugium*

God is our hope and strength, *
   a very present help in trouble.

Therefore will we not fear, though the earth be moved, *
   and though the hills be carried into the midst of the sea;

Though the waters thereof rage and swell, *
   and though the mountains shake at the tempest of the same.

There is a river, the streams whereof make glad the city of God, '
   the holy place of the tabernacle of the Most Highest.

God is in the midst of her,
therefore shall she not be removed; *
   God shall help her, and that right early.

Be still then, and know that I am God; *
   I will be exalted among the nations,
   and I will be exalted in the earth.

The LORD of hosts is with us; *
   the God of Jacob is our refuge.

Psalm 90 *Domine, refugium*

LORD, thou hast been our refuge, *
   from one generation to another.

Before the mountains were brought forth,
or ever the earth and the world were made, *
   thou art God from everlasting, and world without end.

Thou turnest man to destruction; *
   again thou sayest, Come again, ye children of men.

For a thousand years in thy sight are but as yesterday
                 when it is past, *
   and as a watch in the night.

As soon as thou scatterest them they are even as a sleep, *
   and fade away suddenly like the grass.

In the morning it is green, and groweth up; *
   but in the evening it is cut down, dried up, and withered.

For we consume away in thy displeasure, *
   and are afraid at thy wrathful indignation.

Thou hast set our misdeeds before thee,*
   and our secret sins in the light of thy countenance.

For when thou art angry all our days are gone; *
  we bring our years to an end, as it were a tale that is told.

The days of our age are threescore years and ten;
and though men be so strong that they come to fourscore years, *
  yet is their strength then but labor and sorrow,
  so soon passeth it away, and we are gone.

So teach us to number our days, *
  that we may apply our hearts unto wisdom.

Psalm 121   *Levavi oculos*

I will lift up mine eyes unto the hills; *
  from whence cometh my help?

My help cometh even from the LORD, *
  who hath made heaven and earth.

He will not suffer thy foot to be moved, *
  and he that keepeth thee will not sleep.

Behold, he that keepeth Israel *
  shall neither slumber nor sleep.

The LORD himself is thy keeper; *
  the LORD is thy defence upon thy right hand;

So that the sun shall not burn thee by day, *
  neither the moon by night.

The LORD shall preserve thee from all evil; *
  yea, it is even he that shall keep thy soul.

The LORD shall preserve thy going out, and thy coming in, *
  from this time forth for evermore.

Psalm 130   *De profundis*

Out of the deep have I called unto thee, O Lord; *
  Lord, hear my voice.

O let thine ears consider well *
  the voice of my complaint.

If thou, Lord, wilt be extreme to mark what is done amiss, *
  O Lord, who may abide it?

For there is mercy with thee, *
  therefore shalt thou be feared.

I look for the Lord; my soul doth wait for him; *
  in his word is my trust.

My soul fleeth unto the Lord before the morning watch; *
  I say, before the morning watch.

O Israel, trust in the Lord,
for with the Lord there is mercy, *
  and with him is plenteous redemption.

And he shall redeem Israel *
  from all his sins.

Psalm 139   *Domine, probasti*

O Lord, thou hast searched me out, and known me. *
  Thou knowest my down-sitting and mine up-rising;
  thou understandest my thoughts long before.

Thou art about my path, and about my bed, *
  and art acquainted with all my ways.

For lo, there is not a word in my tongue, *
  but thou, O Lord, knowest it altogether.

Thou hast beset me behind and before, *
   and laid thine hand upon me.

Such knowledge is too wonderful and excellent for me; *
   I cannot attain unto it.

Whither shall I go then from thy Spirit? *
   or whither shall I go then from thy presence?

If I climb up into heaven, thou art there; *
   if I go down to hell, thou art there also.

If I take the wings of the morning, *
   and remain in the uttermost parts of the sea;

Even there also shall thy hand lead me, *
   and thy right hand shall hold me.

If I say, Peradventure the darkness shall cover me, *
   then shall my night be turned to day.

Yea, the darkness is no darkness with thee,
but the night is as clear as day; *
   the darkness and light to thee are both alike.

From the New Testament

Romans 8:14-19, 34-35, 37-39 (The glory that shall be revealed)
1 Corinthians 15:20-26, 35-38, 42-44, 53-58 (Raised in incorruption)
2 Corinthians 4:16—5:9 (Things which are not seen are eternal)
1 John 3:1-2 (We shall be like him)
Revelation 7:9-17 (God shall wipe away all tears)
Revelation 21:2-7 (Behold, I make all things new)

*After the New Testament Lesson, a suitable canticle or hymn, or one of
the following Psalms may be sung or said*

Psalm 23   *Dominus regit me*

The LORD is my shepherd; *
  therefore can I lack nothing.

He shall feed me in a green pasture, *
  and lead me forth beside the waters of comfort.

He shall convert my soul, *
  and bring me forth in the paths of righteousness for his
          Name's sake.

Yea, though I walk through the valley of the shadow of death,
I will fear no evil; *
  for thou art with me;
  thy rod and thy staff comfort me.

Thou shalt prepare a table before me in the presence of them
      that trouble me; *
  thou hast anointed my head with oil,
  and my cup shall be full.

Surely thy loving-kindness and mercy shall follow me all the
      days of my life; *
  and I will dwell in the house of the LORD for ever.

Psalm 23   *King James Version*

The LORD is my shepherd; *
  I shall not want.

He maketh me to lie down in green pastures; *
  he leadeth me beside the still waters.

He restoreth my soul; *
  he leadeth me in the paths of righteousness for his
          Name's sake.

Yea, though I walk through the valley of the shadow of death,
I will fear no evil; *
   for thou art with me;
   thy rod and thy staff, they comfort me.

Thou preparest a table before me in the presence of
                              mine enemies; *
   thou anointest my head with oil;
   my cup runneth over.

Surely goodness and mercy shall follow me all the days
                       of my life, *
   and I will dwell in the house of the LORD for ever.

Psalm 27   *Dominus illuminatio*

The LORD is my light and my salvation;
whom then shall I fear? *
   the LORD is the strength of my life;
   of whom then shall I be afraid?

One thing have I desired of the LORD, which I will require, *
   even that I may dwell in the house of the LORD all the
                       days of my life,
   to behold the fair beauty of the LORD, and to visit his temple.

For in the time of trouble he shall hide me in his tabernacle; *
   yea, in the secret place of his dwelling shall he hide me,
   and set me up upon a rock of stone.

And now shall he lift up mine head *
   above mine enemies round about me.

Therefore will I offer in his dwelling an oblation with
                       great gladness; *
   I will sing and speak praises unto the LORD.

Hearken unto my voice, O LORD, when I cry unto thee; *
  have mercy upon me, and hear me.

  My heart hath talked of thee, Seek ye my face. *
    Thy face, LORD, will I seek.

  O hide not thou thy face from me, *
    nor cast thy servant away in displeasure.

  I should utterly have fainted, *
    but that I believe verily to see the goodness of the LORD in
        the land of the living.

  O tarry thou the LORD's leisure; *
    be strong, and he shall comfort thine heart;
    and put thou thy trust in the LORD.

Psalm 106   *Confitemini Domino*

O give thanks unto the LORD, for he is gracious, *
  and his mercy endureth for ever.

Who can express the noble acts of the LORD, *
  or show forth all his praise?

Blessed are they that alway keep judgment, *
  and do righteousness.

Remember me, O LORD, according to the favor that thou
        bearest unto thy people; *
  O visit me with thy salvation;

That I may see the felicity of thy chosen, *
  and rejoice in the gladness of thy people,
  and give thanks with thine inheritance.

Psalm 116 *Dilexi, quoniam*

My delight is in the LORD, *
  because he hath heard the voice of my prayer;

Because he hath inclined his ear unto me, *
  therefore will I call upon him as long as I live.

The snares of death compassed me round about, *
  and the pains of hell gat hold upon me.

I found trouble and heaviness;
then called I upon the Name of the LORD; *
  O LORD, I beseech thee, deliver my soul.

Gracious is the LORD, and righteous; *
  yea, our God is merciful.

The LORD preserveth the simple; *
  I was in misery, and he helped me.

Turn again then unto thy rest, O my soul, *
  for the LORD hath rewarded thee.

And why? thou hast delivered my soul from death, *
  mine eyes from tears, and my feet from falling.

I will walk before the LORD *
  in the land of the living.

I will pay my vows now in the presence of all his people; *
  right dear in the sight of the LORD is the death of his saints.

The Gospel

Then, all standing, the Deacon or Minister appointed reads the Gospel, first saying

> The Holy Gospel of our Lord Jesus Christ
> according to John.

People Glory be to thee, O Lord.

John 5:24-27 (He that believeth hath everlasting life)
John 6:37-40 (All that the Father giveth me shall come to me)
John 10:11-16 (I am the good shepherd)
John 11:21-27 (I am the resurrection and the life)
John 14:1-6 (In my Father's house are many mansions)

At the end of the Gospel, the Reader says

> The Gospel of the Lord.
People   Praise be to thee, O Christ.

A homily may be preached, the people being seated.

The Apostles' Creed may be said, all standing.

If there is not to be a Communion, the Lord's Prayer is said here, and the service continues with the following prayer of intercession, or with one or more suitable prayers (see pages . 21-23).

When there is a Communion, the following serves for the Prayers of the People.

The People respond to every petition with Amen.

The Deacon or other leader says

In peace, let us pray to the Lord.

Almighty God, who hast knit together thine elect in one communion and fellowship, in the mystical body of thy Son Christ our Lord: Grant, we beseech thee, to thy whole Church in paradise and on earth, thy light and thy peace. *Amen.*

Grant that all who have been baptized into Christ's death and resurrection may die to sin and rise to newness of life, and that through the grave and gate of death we may pass with him to our joyful resurrection. *Amen.*

Grant to us who are still in our pilgrimage, and who walk as yet by faith, that thy Holy Spirit may lead us in holiness and righteousness all our days. *Amen.*

Grant to thy faithful people pardon and peace, that we may be cleansed from all our sins, and serve thee with a quiet mind. *Amen.*

Grant to all who mourn a sure confidence in thy fatherly care, that, casting all their grief on thee, they may know the consolation of thy love. *Amen.*

Give courage and faith to those who are bereaved, that they may have strength to meet the days ahead in the comfort of a reasonable and holy hope, in the joyful expectation of eternal life with those they love. *Amen.*

Help us, we pray, in the midst of things we cannot understand, to believe and trust in the communion of saints, the forgiveness of sins, and the resurrection to life everlasting. *Amen.*

Grant us grace to entrust N. to thy never-failing love; receive *him* into the arms of thy mercy, and remember *him* according to the favor which thou bearest unto thy people. *Amen.*

Grant that, increasing in knowledge and love of thee, *he* may go from strength to strength in the life of perfect service in thy heavenly kingdom. *Amen.*

Grant us, with all who have died in the hope of the resurrection, to have our consummation and bliss in thy eternal and everlasting glory, and, with [blessed N. and] all thy saints, to receive the crown of life which thou dost promise to all who share in the victory of thy Son Jesus Christ; who liveth and reigneth with thee and the Holy Spirit, one God, for ever and ever. *Amen.*

When there is no Communion, the service continues with the Commendation, or with the Committal.

At the Eucharist

The service continues with the Peace and the Offertory on page 40 or 48.

Preface of the Commemoration of the Dead

In place of the usual postcommunion prayer, the following is said

Almighty God, we thank thee that in thy great love thou hast
fed us with the spiritual food and drink of the Body and
Blood of thy Son Jesus Christ, and hast given unto us a
foretaste of thy heavenly banquet. Grant that this Sacrament
may be unto us a comfort in affliction, and a pledge of our
inheritance in that kingdom where there is no death, neither
sorrow nor crying, but the fullness of joy with all thy saints;
through Jesus Christ our Savior. *Amen.*

*If the body is not present, the service continues with the [blessing and]
dismissal.*

*Unless the Committal follows immediately in the church, the following
Commendation is used.*

The Commendation

The Celebrant and other ministers take their places at the body.

*This anthem, or some other suitable anthem, or a hymn, may be sung or
said.*

Give rest, O Christ, to thy servant(s) with thy saints,
where sorrow and pain are no more,
neither sighing, but life everlasting.

Thou only art immortal, the creator and maker of mankind;
and we are mortal, formed of the earth, and unto earth shall
we return. For so thou didst ordain when thou createdst me,
saying, "Dust thou art, and unto dust shalt thou return." All

we go down to the dust; yet even at the grave we make
our song: Alleluia, alleluia, alleluia.

Give rest, O Christ, to thy servant(s) with thy saints,
where sorrow and pain are no more,
neither sighing, but life everlasting.

The Celebrant, facing the body, says

Into thy hands, O merciful Savior, we commend thy servant
N. Acknowledge, we humbly beseech thee, a sheep of thine
own fold, a lamb of thine own flock, a sinner of thine own
redeeming. Receive *him* into the arms of thy mercy, into the
blessed rest of everlasting peace, and into the glorious
company of the saints in light. *Amen.*

The Celebrant, or the Bishop if present, may then bless the people, and a
Deacon or other Minister may dismiss them, saying

Let us go forth in the name of Christ.
Thanks be to God.

As the body is borne from the church, a hymn, or one or more of these
anthems may be sung or said

Christ is risen from the dead, trampling down death by death,
and giving life to those in the tomb.

The Sun of Righteousness is gloriously risen, giving light to
those who sat in darkness and in the shadow of death.

The Lord will guide our feet into the way of peace, having
taken away the sin of the world.

Christ will open the kingdom of heaven to all who believe in
his Name, saying, Come, O blessed of my Father; inherit the
kingdom prepared for you.

Into paradise may the angels lead thee; and at thy coming may the martyrs receive thee, and bring thee into the holy city Jerusalem.

or one of these Canticles

The Song of Zechariah, *Benedictus*
The Song of Simeon, *Nunc dimittis*
Christ our Passover, *Pascha nostrum*

The Committal

The following anthem is sung or said.

In the midst of life we are in death;
of whom may we seek for succor,
but of thee, O Lord,
who for our sins art justly displeased?

Yet, O Lord God most holy, O Lord most mighty,
O holy and most merciful Savior,
deliver us not into the bitter pains of eternal death.

Thou knowest, Lord, the secrets of our hearts;
shut not thy merciful ears to our prayer;
but spare us, Lord most holy, O God most mighty,
O holy and merciful Savior,
thou most worthy Judge eternal.
Suffer us not, at our last hour,
through any pains of death, to fall from thee.

or this

All that the Father giveth me shall come to me;
and him that cometh to me I will in no wise cast out.

He that raised up Jesus from the dead
will also give life to our mortal bodies,
by his Spirit that dwelleth in us.

Wherefore my heart is glad, and my spirit rejoiceth;
my flesh also shall rest in hope.

Thou shalt show me the path of life;
in thy presence is the fullness of joy,
and at thy right hand there is pleasure for evermore.

Then, while earth is cast upon the coffin, the Celebrant says these words

In sure and certain hope of the resurrection to eternal life
through our Lord Jesus Christ, we commend to Almighty
God our *brother* N; and we commit *his* body to the ground;*
earth to earth, ashes to ashes, dust to dust. The Lord bless
him and keep *him*, the Lord make his face to shine upon *him*
and be gracious unto *him*, the Lord lift up his countenance
upon *him* and give *him* peace. *Amen.*

* *Or* the deep, *or* the elements, *or* its resting place.

The Celebrant says

The Lord be with you.
People   And with thy spirit.
Celebrant Let us pray.

Celebrant and People

Our Father, who art in heaven,
   hallowed be thy Name,
   thy kingdom come,
   thy will be done,
      on earth as it is in heaven.
Give us this day our daily bread.

And forgive us our trespasses,
   as we forgive those who trespass against us.
And lead us not into temptation,
   but deliver us from evil.
For thine is the kingdom, and the power, and the glory,
   for ever and ever. *Amen.*

Then the Celebrant may say

O Almighty God, the God of the spirits of all flesh, who by a voice from heaven didst proclaim, Blessed are the dead who die in the Lord: Multiply, we beseech thee, to those who rest in Jesus the manifold blessings of thy love, that the good work which thou didst begin in them may be made perfect unto the day of Jesus Christ. And of thy mercy, O heavenly Father, grant that we, who now serve thee on earth, may at last, together with them, be partakers of the inheritance of the saints in light; for the sake of thy Son Jesus Christ our Lord. *Amen.*

In place of this prayer, or in addition to it, the Celebrant may use any of the Additional Prayers.

Then may be said

Rest eternal grant to *him*, O Lord:
And let light perpetual shine upon him.

May *his* soul, and the souls of all the departed,
through the mercy of God, rest in peace. *Amen.*

The Celebrant dismisses the people with these words

The God of peace, who brought again from the dead our Lord Jesus Christ, the great Shepherd of the sheep, through the blood of the everlasting covenant: Make you perfect in every good work to do his will, working in you that which is well pleasing in his sight; through Jesus Christ, to whom be glory for ever and ever. *Amen.*

The Consecration of a Grave

If the grave is in a place that has not previously been set apart for Christian burial, the Priest may use the following prayer, either before the service of Committal or at some other convenient time

O God, whose blessed Son was laid in a sepulcher in the garden: Bless, we pray, this grave, and grant that *he* whose body is (is to be) buried here may dwell with Christ in paradise, and may come to thy heavenly kingdom; through thy Son Jesus Christ our Lord. *Amen.*

Additional Prayers

Almighty and everlasting God, we yield unto thee most high praise and hearty thanks for the wonderful grace and virtue declared in all thy saints, who have been the choice vessels of thy grace, and the lights of the world in their several generations; most humbly beseeching thee to give us grace so to follow the example of their steadfastness in thy faith, and obedience to thy holy commandments, that at the day of the general resurrection, we, with all those who are of the mystical body of thy Son, may be set on his right hand, and hear that his most joyful voice: "Come, ye blessed of my Father, inherit the kingdom prepared for you from the foundation of the world." Grant this, O Father, for the sake of the same thy Son Jesus Christ, our only Mediator and Advocate. *Amen.*

Almighty God, with whom do live the spirits of those who depart hence in the Lord, and with whom the souls of the faithful, after they are delivered from the burden of the flesh, are in joy and felicity: We give thee hearty thanks for the good examples of all those thy servants, who, having finished their course in faith, do now rest from their labors. And we beseech thee that we, with all those who are departed in the true faith of thy holy Name, may have our perfect consummation and bliss, both in body and soul, in thy eternal and everlasting glory; through Jesus Christ our Lord. *Amen.*

Into thy hands, O Lord, we commend thy servant *N.*, our dear *brother*, as into the hands of a faithful Creator and most merciful Savior, beseeching thee that *he* may be precious in thy sight. Wash *him*, we pray thee, in the blood of that immaculate Lamb that was slain to take away the sins of the world; that, whatsoever defilements *he* may have contracted in the midst of this earthly life being purged and done away, *he* may be presented pure and without spot before thee; through the merits of Jesus Christ thine only Son our Lord. *Amen.*

Remember thy servant, O Lord, according to the favor which thou bearest unto thy people; and grant that, increasing in knowledge and love of thee, *he* may go from strength to strength in the life of perfect service in thy heavenly kingdom; through Jesus Christ our Lord. *Amen.*

Almighty God, our heavenly Father, in whose hands are the living and the dead: We give thee thanks for all thy servants who have laid down their lives in the service of our country. Grant to them thy mercy and the light of thy presence; and give us such a lively sense of thy righteous will, that the work which thou hast begun in them may be perfected; through Jesus Christ thy Son our Lord. *Amen.*

O God, whose days are without end, and whose mercies cannot be numbered: Make us, we beseech thee, deeply sensible of the shortness and uncertainty of life; and let thy Holy Spirit lead us in holiness and righteousness all our days; that, when we shall have served thee in our generation, we may be gathered unto our fathers, having the testimony of a good conscience; in the communion of the Catholic Church; in the confidence of a certain faith; in the comfort of a reasonable, religious, and holy hope; in favor with thee our God; and in perfect charity with the world. All which we ask through Jesus Christ our Lord. *Amen.*

O God, the King of saints, we praise and magnify thy holy Name for all thy servants who have finished their course in thy faith and fear; for the blessed Virgin Mary; for the holy patriarchs, prophets, apostles, and martyrs; and for all other thy righteous servants, known to us and unknown; and we beseech thee that, encouraged by their examples, aided by their prayers, and strengthened by their fellowship, we also may be partakers of the inheritance of the saints in light; through the merits of thy Son Jesus Christ our Lord. *Amen.*

O Lord Jesus Christ, Son of the living God, we pray thee to set thy passion, cross, and death, between thy judgment and our souls, now and in the hour of our death. Give mercy and grace to the living, pardon and rest to the dead, to thy holy Church peace and concord, and to us sinners everlasting life and glory; who with the Father and the Holy Spirit livest and reignest, one God, now and for ever. *Amen.*

Almighty God, Father of mercies and giver of all comfort: Deal graciously, we pray thee, with all those who mourn, that casting every care on thee, they may know the consolation of thy love; through Jesus Christ our Lord. *Amen.*

The Burial of the Dead:
Rite Two

All stand while one or more of the following anthems is sung or said.
A hymn, psalm, or some other suitable anthem may be sung instead.

I am Resurrection and I am Life, says the Lord.
Whoever has faith in me shall have life,
even though he die.
And everyone who has life,
and has committed himself to me in faith,
shall not die for ever.

As for me, I know that my Redeemer lives
and that at the last he will stand upon the earth.
After my awaking, he will raise me up;
and in my body I shall see God.
I myself shall see, and my eyes behold him
who is my friend and not a stranger.

For none of us has life in himself,
and none becomes his own master when he dies.
For if we have life, we are alive in the Lord,
and if we die, we die in the Lord.
So, then, whether we live or die,
we are the Lord's possession.

Happy from now on
are those who die in the Lord!
So it is, says the Spirit,
for they rest from their labors.

Or else this anthem

In the midst of life we are in death;
from whom can we seek help?
From you alone, O Lord,
who by our sins are justly angered.

Holy God, Holy and Mighty,
Holy and merciful Savior,
deliver us not into the bitterness of eternal death.

Lord, you know the secrets of our hearts;
shut not your ears to our prayers,
but spare us, O Lord.

Holy God, Holy and Mighty,
Holy and merciful Savior,
deliver us not into the bitterness of eternal death.

O worthy and eternal Judge,
do not let the pains of death
turn us away from you at our last hour.

Holy God, Holy and Mighty,
Holy and merciful Savior,
deliver us not into the bitterness of eternal death.

When all are in place, the Celebrant may address the congregation,
acknowledging briefly the purpose of their gathering, and bidding their
prayers for the deceased and the bereaved.

The Lord be with you.
People   And also with you.
Celebrant Let us pray.

Silence may be kept; after which the Celebrant says one of the following Collects

At the Burial of an Adult

O God, who by the glorious resurrection of your Son Jesus Christ destroyed death, and brought life and immortality to light: Grant that your servant N., being raised with him, may know the strength of his presence, and rejoice in his eternal glory; who with you and the Holy Spirit lives and reigns, one God, for ever and ever. *Amen.*

or this

O God, whose mercies cannot be numbered: Accept our prayers on behalf of your servant N., and grant *him* an entrance into the land of light and joy, in the fellowship of your saints; through Jesus Christ our Lord, who lives and reigns with you and the Holy Spirit, one God, now and for ever. *Amen.*

or this

O God of grace and glory, we remember before you this day our brother (sister) N. We thank you for giving *him* to us, *his* family and friends, to know and to love as a companion on our earthly pilgrimage. In your boundless compassion, console us who mourn. Give us faith to see in death the gate of eternal life, so that in quiet confidence we may continue our course on earth, until, by your call, we are reunited with those who have gone before; through Jesus Christ our Lord. *Amen.*

At the Burial of a Child

O God, whose beloved Son took children into his arms and blessed them: Give us grace to entrust N., to your never-failing care and love, and bring us all to your heavenly kingdom; through Jesus Christ our Lord, who lives and reigns with you and the Holy Spirit, one God, now and for ever. *Amen.*

The Celebrant may add the following prayer

Most merciful God, whose wisdom is beyond our understanding, deal graciously with NN. in *their* grief. Surround *them* with your love, that *they* may not be overwhelmed by *their* loss, but have confidence in your goodness, and strength to meet the days to come; through Jesus Christ our Lord. *Amen.*

The people sit.

One or more of the following passages from Holy Scripture is read. If there is to be a Communion, a passage from the Gospel always concludes the Readings.

The Liturgy of the Word

From the Old Testament

Isaiah 25:6-9 (He will swallow up death for ever)
Isaiah 61:1-3 (To comfort those who mourn)
Lamentations 3:22-26, 31-33 (The Lord is good to those who wait for him)
Wisdom 3:1-5, 9 (The souls of the righteous are in the hands of God)
Job 19:21-27a (I know that my Redeemer lives)

A suitable psalm, hymn, or canticle may follow. The following Psalms are appropriate: 42:1-7; 46:1-6, 11-12; 90:1-12; 121; 130; 139:1-11. *See page 55.*

From the New Testament

Romans 8:14-19, 34-35, 37-39 (The glory that shall be revealed)
1 Corinthians 15:20-26, 35-38, 42-44, 53-58 (The imperishable body)
2 Corinthians 4:16—5:9 (Things that are unseen are eternal)
1 John 3:1-2 (We shall be like him)
Revelation 7:9-17 (God will wipe away every tear)
Revelation 21:2-7 (Behold, I make all things new)

*A suitable psalm, hymn, or canticle may follow. The following
Psalms are appropriate:* 23; 27:1, 5-12, 17-18; 106:1-5; 116:1-8, 12-13.
See page 60.

The Gospel

*Then, all standing, the Deacon or Minister appointed reads the Gospel,
first saying*

> The Holy Gospel of our Lord Jesus Christ
> according to John.
People Glory to you, Lord Christ.

John 5:24-27 (He who believes has everlasting life)
John 6:37-40 (All that the Father gives me will come to me)
John 10:11-16 (I am the good shepherd)
John 11:21-27 (I am the resurrection and the life)
John 14:1-6 (In my Father's house are many rooms)

At the end of the Gospel, the Reader says

> The Gospel of the Lord.
People Praise to you, Lord Christ.

*Here there may be a homily by the Celebrant, or a member of the family,
or a friend.*

The Apostles' Creed may then be said, all standing. The Celebrant may introduce the Creed with these or similar words

In the assurance of eternal life given at Baptism, let us proclaim our faith and say,

Celebrant and People

I believe in God, the Father almighty,
    creator of heaven and earth.

I believe in Jesus Christ, his only Son, our Lord.
    He was conceived by the power of the Holy Spirit
        and born of the Virgin Mary.
    He suffered under Pontius Pilate,
        was crucified, died, and was buried.
    He descended to the dead.
    On the third day he rose again.
    He ascended into heaven,
        and is seated at the right hand of the Father.
    He will come again to judge the living and the dead.

I believe in the Holy Spirit,
    the holy catholic Church,
    the communion of saints,
    the forgiveness of sins,
    the resurrection of the body,
    and the life everlasting. Amen.

If there is not to be a Communion, the Lord's Prayer is said here, and the service continues with the Prayers of the People, or with one or more suitable prayers (see pages 37-39).

When there is a Communion, the following form of the Prayers of the People is used, or else the form on page 14.

For our brother (sister) N., let us pray to our Lord Jesus Christ who said," I am Resurrection and I am Life."

Lord, you consoled Martha and Mary in their distress; draw near to us who mourn for N., and dry the tears of those who weep.
Hear us, Lord.

You wept at the grave of Lazarus, your friend; comfort us in our sorrow.
Hear us, Lord.

You raised the dead to life; give to our brother (sister) eternal life.
Hear us, Lord.

You promised paradise to the thief who repented; bring our brother (sister) to the joys of heaven.
Hear us, Lord.

Our brother (sister) was washed in Baptism and anointed with the Holy Spirit; give *him* fellowship with all your saints.
Hear us, Lord.

He was nourished with your Body and Blood; grant *him* a place at the table in your heavenly kingdom.
Hear us, Lord.

Comfort us in our sorrows at the death of our brother (sister); let our faith be our consolation, and eternal life our hope.

Silence may be kept.

The Celebrant concludes with one of the following or some other prayer

Lord Jesus Christ, we commend to you our brother (sister) *N.*, who was reborn by water and the Spirit in Holy Baptism. Grant that *his* death may recall to us your victory over death, and be an occasion for us to renew our trust in your Father's love. Give us, we pray, the faith to follow where you have led the way; and where you live and reign with the Father and the Holy Spirit, to the ages of ages. *Amen.*

or this

Father of all, we pray to you for *N.*, and for all those whom we love but see no longer. Grant to them eternal rest. Let light perpetual shine upon them. May *his* soul and the souls of all the departed, through the mercy of God, rest in peace. *Amen.*

When there is no Communion, the service continues with the Commendation, or with the Committal.

At the Eucharist.

The service continues with the Peace and the Offertory on page 4 0 or 4 8

Preface of the Commemoration of the Dead

In place of the usual postcommunion prayer, the following is said

Almighty God, we thank you that in your great love you have fed us with the spiritual food and drink of the Body and Blood of your Son Jesus Christ, and have given us a foretaste of your heavenly banquet. Grant that this Sacrament may be to us a comfort in affliction, and a pledge of our inheritance in that kingdom where there is no death, neither sorrow nor crying, but the fullness of joy with all your saints; through Jesus Christ our Savior. *Amen.*

If the body is not present, the service continues with the (blessing and) dismissal.

Unless the Committal follows immediately in the church, the following Commendation is used.

The Commendation

The Celebrant and other ministers take their places at the body.

This anthem, or some other suitable anthem, or a hymn, may be sung or said

Give rest, O Christ, to your servant(s) with your saints,
where sorrow and pain are no more,
neither sighing, but life everlasting.

You only are immortal, the creator and maker of mankind; and we are mortal, formed of the earth, and to earth shall we return. For so did you ordain when you created me, saying, "You are dust, and to dust you shall return." All of us go down to the dust; yet even at the grave we make our song: Alleluia, alleluia, alleluia.

Give rest, O Christ, to your servant(s) with your saints,
where sorrow and pain are no more,
neither sighing, but life everlasting.

The Celebrant, facing the body, says

Into your hands, O merciful Savior, we commend your servant N. Acknowledge, we humbly beseech you, a sheep of your own fold, a lamb of your own flock, a sinner of your own redeeming. Receive *him* into the arms of your mercy, into the blessed rest of everlasting peace, and into the glorious company of the saints in light. *Amen.*

The Celebrant, or the Bishop if present, may then bless the people, and a Deacon or other Minister may dismiss them, saying

Let us go forth in the name of Christ.
Thanks be to God.

As the body is borne from the church, a hymn, or one or more of these anthems may be sung or said

Christ is risen from the dead, trampling down death by death, and giving life to those in the tomb.

The Sun of Righteousness is gloriously risen, giving light to those who sat in darkness and in the shadow of death.

The Lord will guide our feet into the way of peace, having taken away the sin of the world.

Christ will open the kingdom of heaven to all who believe in his Name, saying, Come, O blessed of my Father; inherit the kingdom prepared for you.

Into paradise may the angels lead you. At your coming may the martyrs receive you, and bring you into the holy city Jerusalem.

or one of these Canticles,

The Song of Zechariah, *Benedictus*
The Song of Simeon, *Nunc dimittis*
Christ our Passover, *Pascha nostrum*

The Committal

The following anthem or one of those on pages 25 - 26 is sung or said

Everyone the Father gives to me will come to me;
I will never turn away anyone who believes in me.

He who raised Jesus Christ from the dead
will also give new life to our mortal bodies
through his indwelling Spirit.

My heart, therefore, is glad, and my spirit rejoices;
my body also shall rest in hope.

You will show me the path of life;
in your presence there is fullness of joy,
and in your right hand are pleasures for evermore.

Then, while earth is cast upon the coffin, the Celebrant says these words

In sure and certain hope of the resurrection to eternal life
through our Lord Jesus Christ, we commend to Almighty
God our *brother N.*, and we commit *his* body to the ground;*
earth to earth, ashes to ashes, dust to dust. The Lord bless
him and keep *him*, the Lord make his face to shine upon *him*
and be gracious to *him*, the Lord lift up his countenance upon
him and give *him* peace. *Amen.*

*Or the deep, or the elements, or its resting place.

The Celebrant says

	The Lord be with you.
People	And also with you.
Celebrant	Let us pray.

Our Father, who art in heaven,
   hallowed be thy Name,
   thy kingdom come,
   thy will be done,
     on earth as it is in heaven.
Give us this day our daily bread.
And forgive us our trespasses,
   as we forgive those
    who trespass against us.
And lead us not into temptation,
   but deliver us from evil.
For thine is the kingdom,
   and the power, and the glory,
   for ever and ever. Amen.

Our Father in heaven,
   hallowed be your Name,
   your kingdom come,
   your will be done,
     on earth as in heaven.
Give us today our daily bread.
Forgive us our sins
   as we forgive those
    who sin against us.
Save us from the time of trial,
   and deliver us from evil.
For the kingdom, the power,
   and the glory are yours,
   now and for ever. Amen.

Other prayers may be added.

Then may be said

Rest eternal grant to *him*, O Lord;
And let light perpetual shine upon him.

May *his* soul, and the souls of all the departed,
through the mercy of God, rest in peace. *Amen.*

The Celebrant dismisses the people with these words

        Alleluia. Christ is risen.
People   The Lord is risen indeed. Alleluia.
Celebrant Let us go forth in the name of Christ.
People   Thanks be to God.

or with the following

The God of peace, who brought again from the dead our Lord Jesus Christ, the great Shepherd of the sheep, through the blood of the everlasting covenant: Make you perfect in every good work to do his will, working in you that which is well-pleasing in his sight; through Jesus Christ, to whom be glory for ever and ever. *Amen.*

The Consecration of a Grave

If the grave is in a place that has not previously been set apart for Christian burial, the Priest may use the following prayer, either before the service of Committal or at some other convenient time

O God, whose blessed Son was laid in a sepulcher in the garden: Bless, we pray, this grave, and grant that *he* whose body is (is to be) buried here may dwell with Christ in paradise, and may come to your heavenly kingdom; through your Son Jesus Christ our Lord. *Amen.*

Additional prayers

Almighty God, with whom still live the spirits of those who die in the Lord, and with whom the souls of the faithful are in joy and felicity: We give you heartfelt thanks for the good examples of all your servants, who, having finished their course in faith, now find rest and refreshment. May we, with all who have died in the true faith of your holy Name, have perfect fulfillment and bliss in your eternal and everlasting glory, through Jesus Christ our Lord. *Amen.*

O God, whose days are without end, and whose mercies cannot be numbered: Make us, we pray, deeply aware of the shortness and uncertainty of human life; and let your Holy Spirit lead us in holiness and righteousness all our days; that, when we shall have served you in our generation, we may be gathered to our ancestors, having the testimony of a good conscience, in the communion of the Catholic Church, in the confidence of a certain faith, in the comfort of a religious and holy hope, in favor with you, our God, and in perfect charity with the world. All this we ask through Jesus Christ our Lord. *Amen.*

O God, the King of saints, we praise and glorify your holy Name for all your servants who have finished their course in your faith and fear: for the blessed Virgin Mary; for the holy patriarchs, prophets, apostles, and martyrs; and for all your other righteous servants, known to us and unknown; and we pray that, encouraged by their examples, aided by their prayers, and strengthened by their fellowship, we also may be partakers of the inheritance of the saints in light; through the merits of your Son Jesus Christ our Lord. *Amen.*

Lord Jesus Christ, by your death you took away the sting of death: Grant to us your servants so to follow in faith where you have led the way, that we may at length fall asleep peacefully in you and wake up in your likeness; for your tender mercies' sake. *Amen.*

Father of all, we pray to you for those we love, but see no longer: Grant them your peace; let light perpetual shine upon them; and, in your loving wisdom and almighty power, work in them the good purpose of your perfect will; through Jesus Christ our Lord. *Amen.*

Merciful God, Father of our Lord Jesus Christ who is the Resurrection and the Life: Raise us, we humbly pray, from the death of sin to the life of righteousness; that when we depart this life we may rest in him, and at the resurrection receive that blessing which your well-beloved Son shall then pronounce:"Come, you blessed of my Father, receive the kingdom prepared for you from the beginning of the world." Grant this, O merciful Father, through Jesus Christ, our Mediator and Redeemer. *Amen.*

Grant, O Lord, to all who are bereaved the spirit of faith and courage, that they may have strength to meet the days to come with steadfastness and patience; not sorrowing as those without hope, but in thankful remembrance of your great goodness, and in the joyful expectation of eternal life with those they love. And this we ask in the Name of Jesus Christ our Savior. *Amen.*

Almighty God, Father of mercies and giver of comfort: Deal graciously, we pray, with all who mourn; that, casting all their care on you, they may know the consolation of your love; through Jesus Christ our Lord. *Amen.*

The Holy Eucharist: Rite One

The Peace

All stand. The Celebrant says to the people

        The peace of the Lord be always with you.
People   And with thy spirit.

Then the Ministers and People may greet one another in the name of the Lord.

The Holy Communion

The Celebrant may begin the Offertory with some appropriate sentence of Scripture.

During the Offertory, a hymn, psalm, or anthem may be sung.

Representatives of the congregation bring the people's offerings of bread and wine, and money or other gifts, to the deacon or celebrant. The people stand while the offerings are presented and placed on the Altar.

The Great Thanksgiving

Eucharistic Prayer I

The people remain standing. The Celebrant, whether bishop or priest, faces them and sings or says

        The Lord be with you.
People   And with thy spirit.
Celebrant Lift up your hearts.
People   We lift them up unto the Lord.
Celebrant Let us give thanks unto our Lord God.
People   It is meet and right so to do.

It is very meet, right, and our bounden duty, that we should at all times, and in all places, give thanks unto thee, O Lord, holy Father, almighty, everlasting God.

Through Jesus Christ our Lord; who rose victorious from the dead, and doth comfort us with the blessed hope of everlasting life; for to thy faithful people, O Lord, life is changed, not ended; and when our mortal body doth lie in death, there is prepared for us a dwelling place eternal in the heavens.

Therefore with Angels and Archangels, and with all the company of heaven, we laud and magnify thy glorious Name; evermore praising thee, and saying,

Celebrant and People

Holy, holy, holy, Lord God of Hosts:
Heaven and earth are full of thy glory.
Glory be to thee, O Lord Most High.

Here may be added

Blessed is he that cometh in the name of the Lord.
Hosanna in the highest.

The people kneel or stand.

Then the Celebrant continues

All glory be to thee, Almighty God, our heavenly Father, for that thou, of thy tender mercy, didst give thine only Son Jesus Christ to suffer death upon the cross for our redemption; who made there, by his one oblation of himself once offered, a full, perfect, and sufficient sacrifice, oblation, and satisfaction, for the sins of the whole world; and did institute, and in his holy Gospel command us to continue, a perpetual memory of that his precious death and sacrifice, until his coming again.

At the following words concerning the bread, the Celebrant is to hold it, or lay a hand upon it; and at the words concerning the cup, to hold or place a hand upon the cup and any other vessel containing wine to be consecrated.

For in the night in which he was betrayed, he took bread; and when he had given thanks, he brake it, and gave it to his disciples, saying, "Take, eat, this is my Body, which is given for you. Do this in remembrance of me."

Likewise, after supper, he took the cup; and when he had given thanks, he gave it to them, saying, "Drink ye all of this; for this is my Blood of the New Testament, which is shed for you, and for many, for the remission of sins. Do this, as oft as ye shall drink it, in remembrance of me."

Wherefore, O Lord and heavenly Father, according to the institution of thy dearly beloved Son our Savior Jesus Christ, we, thy humble servants, do celebrate and make here before thy divine Majesty, with these thy holy gifts, which we now offer unto thee, the memorial thy Son hath commanded us to make; having in remembrance his blessed passion and precious death, his mighty resurrection and glorious ascension; rendering unto thee most hearty thanks for the innumerable benefits procured unto us by the same.

And we most humbly beseech thee, O merciful Father, to hear us; and, of thy almighty goodness, vouchsafe to bless and sanctify, with thy Word and Holy Spirit, these thy gifts and creatures of bread and wine; that we, receiving them according to thy Son our Savior Jesus Christ's holy institution, in remembrance of his death and passion, may be partakers of his most blessed Body and Blood.

And we earnestly desire thy fatherly goodness mercifully to accept this our sacrifice of praise and thanksgiving; most humbly beseeching thee to grant that, by the merits and death of thy Son Jesus Christ, and through faith in his blood, we, and all thy whole Church, may obtain remission of our sins, and all other benefits of his passion.

And here we offer and present unto thee, O Lord, our selves, our souls and bodies, to be a reasonable, holy, and living sacrifice unto thee; humbly beseeching thee that we, and all others who shall be partakers of this Holy Communion, may worthily receive the most precious Body and Blood of thy Son Jesus Christ, be filled with thy grace and heavenly benediction, and made one body with him, that he may dwell in us, and we in him.

And although we are unworthy, through our manifold sins, to offer unto thee any sacrifice, yet we beseech thee to accept this our bounden duty and service, not weighing our merits, but pardoning our offenses, through Jesus Christ our Lord;

By whom, and with whom, in the unity of the Holy Ghost, all honor and glory be unto thee, O Father Almighty, world without end. *AMEN.*

And now, as our Savior Christ hath taught us, we are bold to say,

People and Celebrant

Our Father, who art in heaven,
   hallowed be thy Name,
   thy kingdom come,
   thy will be done,
      on earth as it is in heaven.
Give us this day our daily bread.
And forgive us our trespasses,

as we forgive those who trespass against us.
And lead us not into temptation,
   but deliver us from evil.
For thine is the kingdom, and the power, and the glory,
   for ever and ever. Amen.

The Breaking of the Bread

The Celebrant breaks the consecrated Bread.

A period of silence is kept.

Then may be sung or said

[Alleluia.] Christ our Passover is sacrificed for us;
Therefore let us keep the feast. [*Alleluia.*]

*In Lent, Alleluia is omitted, and may be omitted at other times
except during Easter Season.*

*The following or some other suitable anthem may be sung or
said here*

O Lamb of God, that takest away the sins of the world,
have mercy upon us.
O Lamb of God, that takest away the sins of the world,
have mercy upon us.
O Lamb of God, that takest away the sins of the world,
grant us thy peace.

*The following prayer may be said. The People may join in
saying this prayer*

We do not presume to come to this thy Table, O merciful
Lord, trusting in our own righteousness, but in thy manifold

and great mercies. We are not worthy so much as to gather up the crumbs under thy Table. But thou art the same Lord whose property is always to have mercy. Grant us therefore, gracious Lord, so to eat the flesh of thy dear Son Jesus Christ, and to drink his blood, that we may evermore dwell in him, and he in us. *Amen.*

Facing the people, the Celebrant may say the following Invitation

The Gifts of God for the People of God.
and may add Take them in remembrance that Christ died for you, and feed on him in your hearts by faith, with thanksgiving.

The ministers receive the Sacrament in both kinds, and then immediately deliver it to the people.

The Bread and the Cup are given to the communicants with these words

The Body of our Lord Jesus Christ, which was given for thee, preserve thy body and soul unto everlasting life. Take and eat this in remembrance that Christ died for thee, and feed on him in thy heart by faith, with thanksgiving.

The Blood of our Lord Jesus Christ, which was shed for thee, preserve thy body and soul unto everlasting life. Drink this in remembrance that Christ's Blood was shed for thee, and be thankful.

or with these words

The Body (Blood) of our Lord Jesus Christ keep you in everlasting life. [*Amen.*]

or with these words

The Body of Christ, the bread of heaven. [*Amen.*]
The Blood of Christ, the cup of salvation. [*Amen.*]

During the ministration of Communion, hymns, psalms, or anthems may be sung.

When necessary, the Celebrant consecrates additional bread and wine.

After Communion, the Celebrant says

Let us pray.

The people may join in saying this prayer

Almighty God, we thank thee that in thy great love thou hast fed us with the spiritual food and drink of the Body and Blood of thy Son Jesus Christ, and hast given unto us a foretaste of thy heavenly banquet. Grant that this Sacrament may be unto us a comfort in affliction, and a pledge of our inheritance in that kingdom where there is no death, neither sorrow nor crying, but the fullness of joy with all thy saints; through Jesus Christ our Savior. Amen.

The service continues with the Commendation and Committal, on page 16 or 33.

If the body is not present, the service continues with the (blessing and) dismissal.

The Bishop when present, or the Priest, gives the blessing

The peace of God, which passeth all understanding, keep your hearts and minds in the knowledge and love of God, and of his Son Jesus Christ our Lord; and the blessing of God Almighty, the Father, the Son, and the Holy Ghost, be amongst you, and remain with you always. *Amen.*

or this

The blessing of God Almighty, the Father, the Son, and

the Holy Spirit, be upon you and remain with you for ever. *Amen.*

The Deacon, or the Celebrant, may dismiss the people with these words

            Let us go forth in the name of Christ.
People   Thanks be to God.

or the following

Deacon   Go in peace to love and serve the Lord.
People   Thanks be to God.

or this

Deacon   Let us go forth into the world, rejoicing
            in the power of the Spirit.
People   Thanks be to God.

or this

Deacon   Let us bless the Lord.
People   Thanks be to God.

From the Easter Vigil through the Day of Pentecost "Alleluia, alleluia" may be added to any of the dismissals.

The People respond   Thanks be to God. Alleluia, alleluia.

The Holy Eucharist: Rite Two

The Peace

All stand. The Celebrant says to the people

The peace of the Lord be always with you.
People   And also with you.

Then the Ministers and People may greet one another in the name of the Lord.

The Holy Communion

The Celebrant may begin the Offertory with some sentence of Scripture.

During the Offertory, a hymn, psalm, or anthem may be sung.

Representatives of the congregation bring the people's offerings of bread and wine, and money or other gifts, to the deacon or celebrant. The people stand while the offerings are presented and placed on the Altar.

The Great Thanksgiving

Eucharistic Prayer A

The people remain standing. The Celebrant, whether bishop or priest, faces them and sings or says

The Lord be with you.
People   And also with you.
Celebrant Lift up your hearts.
People   We lift them to the Lord.

Celebrant Let us give thanks to the Lord our God.
People It is right to give him thanks and praise.

Then, facing the Holy Table, the Celebrant proceeds

It is right, and a good and joyful thing, always and everywhere to give thanks to you, Father Almighty, Creator of heaven and earth.

Through Jesus Christ our Lord, who rose victorious from the dead, and comforts us with the blessed hope of everlasting life. For to your faithful people, O Lord, life is changed, not ended; and when our mortal body lies in death, there is prepared for us a dwelling place eternal in the heavens.

Therefore we praise you, joining our voices with Angels and Archangels and with all the company of heaven, who for ever sing this hymn to proclaim the glory of your Name:

Celebrant and People

Holy, holy, holy Lord, God of power and might, heaven and earth are full of your glory.
   Hosanna in the highest.
Blessed is he who comes in the name of the Lord.
   Hosanna in the highest.

The people stand or kneel.

Then the Celebrant continues

Holy and gracious Father: In your infinite love you made us for yourself; and, when we had fallen into sin and become subject to evil and death, you, in your mercy, sent Jesus Christ, your only and eternal Son, to share our

49

human nature, to live and die as one of us, to reconcile us to you, the God and Father of all.

He stretched out his arms upon the cross, and offered himself, in obedience to your will, a perfect sacrifice for the whole world.

At the following words concerning the bread, the Celebrant is to hold it, or lay a hand upon it; and at the words concerning the cup, to hold or place a hand upon the cup and any other vessel containing wine to be consecrated.

On the night he was handed over to suffering and death, our Lord Jesus Christ took bread; and when he had given thanks to you, he broke it, and gave it to his disciples, and said, "Take, eat: This is my Body, which is given for you. Do this for the remembrance of me."

After supper he took the cup of wine; and when he had given thanks, he gave it to them, and said, "Drink this, all of you: This is my Blood of the new Covenant, which is shed for you and for many for the forgiveness of sins. Whenever you drink it, do this for the remembrance of me."

Therefore we proclaim the mystery of faith:

Celebrant and People

Christ has died.
Christ is risen.
Christ will come again.

The Celebrant continues

We celebrate the memorial of our redemption, O Father, in this sacrifice of praise and thanksgiving. Recalling his death, resurrection, and ascension, we offer you these gifts.

Sanctify them by your Holy Spirit to be for your people
the Body and Blood of your Son, the holy food and drink
of new and unending life in him. Sanctify us also that
we may faithfully receive this holy Sacrament, and serve
you in unity, constancy, and peace; and at the last day
bring us with all your saints into the joy of your eternal
kingdom.

All this we ask through your Son Jesus Christ. By him,
and with him, and in him, in the unity of the Holy Spirit
all honor and glory is yours, Almighty Father, now
and for ever. *Amen.*

And now, as our Savior Christ has taught us, we are bold to say,	As our Savior Christ has taught us, we now pray,

People and Celebrant

Our Father, who art in heaven,
  hallowed be thy Name,
  thy kingdom come,
  thy will be done,
    on earth as it is in heaven.
Give us this day our daily bread.
And forgive us our trespasses,
  as we forgive those
    who trespass against us.
And lead us not into temptation,
  but deliver us from evil.
For thine is the kingdom,
  and the power, and the glory,
  for ever and ever. Amen.
	Our Father in heaven,
	  hallowed be your Name,
	  your kingdom come,
	  your will be done,
	    on earth as in heaven.
	Give us today our daily bread.
	Forgive us our sins
	  as we forgive those
	    ·who sin against us.
	Save us from the time of trial,
	  and deliver us from evil.
	For the kingdom, the power,
	  and the glory are yours,
	  now and for ever. Amen.

The Breaking of the Bread

The Celebrant breaks the consecrated Bread.

A period of silence is kept.

Then may be sung or said

[Alleluia.] Christ our Passover is sacrificed for us;
Therefore let us keep the feast. [Alleluia.]

*In Lent, Alleluia is omitted, and may be omitted at other times
except during Easter Season.*

*In place of, or in addition to, the preceding, some other suitable
anthem may be used.*

Facing the people, the Celebrant says the following Invitation

The Gifts of God for the People of God.
and may add   Take them in remembrance that Christ died
for you, and feed on him in your hearts
by faith, with thanksgiving.

*The ministers receive the Sacrament in both kinds, and then
immediately deliver it to the people.*

*The Bread and the Cup are given to the communicants with
these words*

The Body (Blood) of our Lord Jesus Christ keep you in
everlasting life. *[Amen.]*

or with these words

The Body of Christ, the Bread of heaven. *[Amen.]*
The Blood of Christ, the Cup of salvation. *[Amen.]*

52

During the ministration of Communion, hymns, psalms, or anthems may be sung.

When necessary, the Celebrant consecrates additional bread and wine.

After Communion, the Celebrant says

Let us pray.

Celebrant and People

Almighty God, we thank you that in your great love you have fed us with the spiritual food and drink of the Body and Blood of your Son Jesus Christ, and have given us a foretaste of your heavenly banquet. Grant that this Sacrament may be to us a comfort in affliction, and a pledge of our inheritance in that kingdom where there is no death, neither sorrow nor crying, but the fullness of joy with all your saints; through Jesus Christ our Savior. *Amen.*

The service continues with the Commendation and Committal, on page 16 or 33.

If the body is not present, the service continues with the (blessing and) dismissal.

The Bishop when present, or the Priest, may bless the people.

The Deacon, or the Celebrant, dismisses them with these words

          Let us go forth in the name of Christ.
People   Thanks be to God.

or this

Deacon   Go in peace to love and serve the Lord.
People   Thanks be to God.

or this

Deacon	Let us go forth into the world, rejoicing in the power of the Spirit.
People	Thanks be to God.

or this

Deacon	Let us bless the Lord.
People	Thanks be to God.

From the Easter Vigil through the Day of Pentecost "Alleluia, alleluia" may be added to any of the dismissals.

The People respond   Thanks be to God. Alleluia, alleluia.

Psalms

for use with Burial Rite Two

42 *Quemadmodum*

As the deer longs for the water-brooks, *
   so longs my soul for you, O God.

My soul is athirst for God, athirst for the living God; *
   when shall I come to appear before the presence of God?

My tears have been my food day and night, *
   while all day long they say to me,
  "Where now is your God?"

I pour out my soul when I think on these things: *
   how I went with the multitude and led them into the
           house of God,

With the voice of praise and thanksgiving, *
   among those who keep holy-day.

Why are you so full of heaviness, O my soul? *
   and why are you so disquieted within me?

Put your trust in God; *
   for I will yet give thanks to him,
   who is the help of my countenance, and my God.

46 *Deus noster refugium*

God is our refuge and strength, *
   a very present help in trouble.

Therefore we will not fear, though the earth be moved, *
   and though the mountains be toppled into the
                depths of the sea;

Though its waters rage and foam, *
   and though the mountains tremble at its tumult.

The LORD of hosts is with us; *
   the God of Jacob is our stronghold.

There is a river whose streams make glad the city of God, *
   the holy habitation of the Most High.

God is in the midst of her;
she shall not be overthrown; *
   God shall help her at the break of day.

"Be still, then, and know that I am God; *
   I will be exalted among the nations;
   I will be exalted in the earth."

  The LORD of hosts is with us; *
    the God of Jacob is our stronghold.

90 *Domine, refugium*

Lord, you have been our refuge *
   from one generation to another.

Before the mountains were brought forth,
or the land and the earth were born, *
   from age to age you are God.

You turn us back to the dust and say, *
   "Go back, O child of earth."

For a thousand years in your sight are like yesterday
                when it is past *

and like a watch in the night.

You sweep us away like a dream; *
  we fade away suddenly like the grass.

In the morning it is green and flourishes; *
  in the evening it is dried up and withered.

For we consume away in your displeasure; *
  we are afraid because of your wrathful indignation.

Our iniquities you have set before you, *
  and our secret sins in the light of your countenance.

When you are angry, all our days are gone; *
  we bring our years to an end like a sigh.

The span of our life is seventy years,
perhaps in strength even eighty; *
  yet the sum of them is but labor and sorrow,
  for they pass away quickly and we are gone.

Who regards the power of your wrath? *
  who rightly fears your indignation?

So teach us to number our days *
  that we may apply our hearts to wisdom.

121 *Levavi oculos*

I lift up my eyes to the hills; *
  from where is my help to come?

My help comes from the LORD, *
  the maker of heaven and earth.

He will not let your foot be moved *
  and he who watches over you will not fall asleep.

Behold, he who keeps watch over Israel *
    shall neither slumber nor sleep;

The LORD himself watches over you; *
    the LORD is your shade at your right hand,

So that the sun shall not strike you by day, *
    nor the moon by night.

The LORD shall preserve you from all evil; *
    it is he who shall keep you safe.

The LORD shall watch over your going out and
                    your coming in, *
    from this time forth for evermore.

130   *De profundis*

Out of the depths have I called to you, O LORD;
LORD, hear my voice; *
    let your ears consider well the voice of my supplication.

If you, LORD, were to note what is done amiss, *
    O Lord, who could stand?

For there is forgiveness with you; *
    therefore you shall be feared.

I wait for the LORD; my soul waits for him; *
    in his word is my hope.

My soul waits for the LORD,
more than watchmen for the morning, *
    more than watchmen for the morning.

O Israel, wait for the LORD, *
    for with the LORD there is mercy;

With him there is plenteous redemption, *
    and he shall redeem Israel from all their sins.

139 *Domine, probasti*

LORD, you have searched me out and known me; *
    you know my sitting down and my rising up;
    you discern my thoughts from afar.

You trace my journeys and my resting-places *
    and are acquainted with all my ways.

Indeed, there is not a word on my lips, *
    but you, O LORD, know it altogether.

You press upon me behind and before *
    and lay your hand upon me.

Such knowledge is too wonderful for me; *
    it is so high that I cannot attain to it.

Where can I go then from your Spirit? *
    where can I flee from your presence?

If I climb up to heaven, you are there; *
    if I make the grave my bed, you are there also.

If I take the wings of the morning *
    and dwell in the uttermost parts of the sea,

Even there your hand will lead me *
    and your right hand hold me fast.

If I say, "Surely the darkness will cover me. *
    and the light around me turn to night,"

Darkness is not dark to you;
the night is as bright as the day; *
    darkness and light to you are both alike.

23 *Dominus regit me*

The LORD is my shepherd; *
    I shall not be in want.

He makes me lie down in green pastures *
    and leads me beside still waters.

He revives my soul *
    and guides me along right pathways for his Name's sake.

Though I walk through the valley of the shadow of death,
I shall fear no evil; *
    for you are with me;
    your rod and your staff, they comfort me.

You spread a table before me in the presence of those
               who trouble me; *
    you have anointed my head with oil,
    and my cup is running over.

Surely your goodness and mercy shall follow me all the days
               of my life, *
    and I will dwell in the house of the LORD for ever.

27 *Dominus illuminatio*

The LORD is my light and my salvation;
whom then shall I fear? *
    the LORD is the strength of my life;
    of whom then shall I be afraid?

One thing have I asked of the LORD;
one thing I seek; *
    that I may dwell in the house of the LORD all the days
               of my life;

To behold the fair beauty of the LORD *
  and to seek him in his temple.

For in the day of trouble he shall keep me safe
              in his shelter; *
  he shall hide me in the secrecy of his dwelling
  and set me high upon a rock.

Even now he lifts up my head *
  above my enemies round about me.

Therefore I will offer in his dwelling an oblation
with sounds of great gladness; *
  I will sing and make music to the LORD.

Hearken to my voice, O LORD, when I call; *
  have mercy on me and answer me.

You speak in my heart and say, "Seek my face." *
  Your face, LORD, will I seek.

Hide not your face from me, *
  nor turn away your servant in displeasure.

What if I had not believed
that I should see the goodness of the LORD *
  in the land of the living!

O tarry and await the LORD's pleasure;
be strong, and he shall comfort your heart; *
  wait patiently for the LORD.

106

Confitemini Domino

Hallelujah!
Give thanks to the LORD, for he is good, *
   for his mercy endures for ever.

Who can declare the mighty acts of the LORD *
   or show forth all his praise?

Happy are those who act with justice *
   and always do what is right!

Remember me, O LORD, with the favor you have
               for your people, *
   and visit me with your saving help;

That I may see the prosperity of your elect
and be glad with the gladness of your people, *
   that I may glory with your inheritance.

116 *Dilexi, quoniam*

I love the LORD, because he has heard the voice of
               my supplication, *
   because he has inclined his ear to me whenever
               I called upon him.

The cords of death entangled me;
  the grip of the grave took hold of me; *
   I came to grief and sorrow.

Then I called upon the Name of the LORD: *
  "O LORD, I pray you, save my life."

Gracious is the LORD and righteous; *
    our God is full of compassion.

The LORD watches over the innocent; *
    I was brought very low, and he helped me.

Turn again to your rest, O my soul, *
    for the LORD has treated you well.

For you have rescued my life from death, *
    my eyes from tears, and my feet from stumbling.

I will walk in the presence of the LORD *
    in the land of the living.

I will fulfill my vows to the LORD *
    in the presence of all his people.

Precious in the sight of the LORD *
    is the death of his servants.